AUTHORS UNCOVERED

AUTHORS UNCOVERED

Britain's Favourite Children's Authors

Jack E. Heywood

© Jack E. Heywood, 2021

Published by Vicuña Books UK

A CIP catalogue record for this book is available from the British Library.

ISBN 978-1-7399125-0-5

Book layout and cover design by Clare Brayshaw

Cover images © Vasilyrosca, © Blotty | Dreamstime.com

Prepared and printed by:

York Publishing Services Ltd
64 Hallfield Road
Layerthorpe
York YO31 7ZQ

Tel: 01904 431213

Website: www.yps-publishing.co.uk

Authors Uncovered: Favourite American and Canadian Children's Authors, David Hallam-Jones Vicuña Books UK (Available 2022)

Contents

Foreword

I think that people will enjoy finding out about their favourite authors in Jack's book. I am sure it will inspire lots of kids to read more which is great. I personally read a lot and love it when I can see situations from different people's point of view. Good authors get you to care about things. Reading can help people find their voices to express ideas so that they can work for a better and fairer world.

I am part of a choir called *S.O.S from the Kids* www.sosfromthekids.com We hope to show people how precious planet earth is and how it's in danger so they will want to protect it. I think that Jack's book will show how authors are able to help children understand more about the world we live in and love it even more.

I hope you enjoy it!

Sim Macaulay

Image © Ekaterina Zirina | Dreamstime.com

Introduction

I am a 10-year-old boy from Nottingham, England. I love reading books but realised how little I knew about the writers whose stories I read. I know this is true for most of my friends as well. My grandad, who listens to children reading at my school, noticed the same thing; many of us enjoy reading but we don't always know much about the background of the books or their authors.

As a home-school project during the COVID-19 lockdown in 2020, I worked with my grandad to research and write about different British children's authors. We found it fascinating and decided to turn my project into a book that other children can enjoy and benefit from.

It is usually adults who write books for children, and I wanted to change this and be a child writing for anyone. After all, we are the new generation and have big voices that need to be heard by each other and by adults.

I hope you will find my book interesting and enjoyable, but I also hope it inspires you to find ways of making your ideas heard.

Malorie Blackman

- **Born:** 8th February 1962
- **To:** Present
- **Place of birth:** Clapham, London
- **First book:** *Not So Stupid* (1990)
- **Best-known book:** *Noughts and Crosses* series (2001-2019)

Malorie's parents came from Barbados and settled in South London. Malorie's mum helped her develop a love of reading and she enjoyed visiting her local library and reading books such as *The Chronicles of Narnia*, *Little Women* and *Jane Eyre*.

When she was a teenager her parents separated, and she describes her 13-year-old self as "utterly miserable" saying that she coped by inventing storylines in her head. Although she smiled at everyone, she felt angry and bitter inside and by the time she was in her mid-teens, she felt very hostile towards other people, particularly towards white teenagers. At grammar school she loved English and reading but she was annoyed that there were no stories by black writers or with black characters. It was only her discovery of Alice Walker's book, *The Color Purple*, that made her wonder if she might become a writer in the future.

At the age of 28, after two years of rejections, she was proud to see her first book published. As a black writer she faced lots of opposition from editors, booksellers and librarians, who said, "A white child won't read a book with a black child on the cover" or "White children will find it too difficult to deal with things that matter to black people." However, she explained that her aim was simply to write about issues all humans face.

Since the 1990s, Malorie has written over seventy books for children and young adults, and some of her books have been translated into different languages. Although most of the characters in her books are black, in her *Noughts and Crosses* series she wrote about struggles between white and black people, very successfully explaining racism to readers. In 2008 Malorie was appointed **OBE** for services to children's literature. She has also received many other awards and recognition for her efforts in promoting racial and gender equality. Between 2013 and 2015 she served as the **Children's Laureate**.

Malorie is married to Neil Morrison, a Scot, and their daughter Elizabeth was born in 1995. Malorie has described her attic as her favourite place to write, however she hates to be interrupted, finding that even simple distractions can disturb her thinking.

"What is the most important lesson life has taught me?
When life knocks you down, keep getting up."
Malorie Blackman

Enid Blyton

- **Born:** 11th August 1897
- **Died:** 28th November 1968
- **Place of birth:** East Dulwich, London
- **First book:** *Child Whispers* (1922)
- **Best-known book:** *The Famous Five* series (1942–1963)

Enid's father Thomas was a cutlery salesman and her mother, Theresa, was a **milliner**. She had two younger brothers. Enid and her father spent a lot of time away from their home enjoying nature, art, music, literature and the theatre.

As a child she went to two small private schools including St. Christopher's Secondary School for Girls that had 50 pupils. Not only was she good at art and English but she was also the captain of the lacrosse team and a champion tennis player. As head girl, she and two other pupils even produced their own magazine.

When she was 13 years old, her parents separated and, as a way of helping herself cope, Enid spent hours on her own in her bedroom writing. She had already made up her mind that she wanted to become a writer, and when she was 14 years old, she entered a children's poetry competition. The competition organiser was so impressed with her efforts that he offered to pay for her verses to be printed. In 1916, Miss Blyton trained as a teacher. Then, although she taught at a boys' **prep school** for a short time, she quickly became a governess to a wealthy couple and home-schooled their four sons. By this time, her writing was improving and journals for schoolteachers were accepting her articles.

In time, she become best known as the writer of over 700 children's books, including series on Noddy, the Famous Five, Malory Towers and the Secret Seven. Although some of her children's stories have been criticised by adults, she is still regularly voted the UK's best-loved author and, according to UNESCO, the world's fourth most translated author. More than 500 million copies of her books have been sold in over 40 languages and many of her books have been made into plays, films and TV series. Enid married twice and had two daughters with her first husband. She spent the last few months of her life in a nursing home in Hampstead, North London, and died at the age of 71 years.

"The best way to treat obstacles is to use them as stepping-stones. Laugh at them, tread on them, and let them lead you to something better."

Enid Blyton

Lewis Carroll

- **Born:** 27th January 1832
- **Died:** 14th January 1898
- **Place of birth:** Daresbury, Cheshire
- **First book:** *Alice's Adventures in Wonderland* (1865)
- **Best-known book:** *Alice's Adventures in Wonderland* (1865)

Born Charles Lutwidge Dodgson but better known by his **pen name** Lewis Carroll, he was part of a large, busy family. His father was a Church of England vicar. Carroll was a clever child, with a slight stammer and was deaf in one ear due to a childhood infectious disease. He was home-schooled until the age of twelve when he attended Richmond Grammar School for eighteen months and then he was a boarder at Rugby School for three years. Lewis Carroll used his fists to protect smaller boys from bullying.

In 1851 he moved to Christ Church College, Oxford University, to study but only stayed for two days because his mother had died of "inflammation of the brain". After he returned, he earned a first-class honours maths degree. In 1855 he became a maths lecturer in the same university, a job that he kept for 26 years. Carroll had written poems and stories from a young age and, in addition to his teaching, he continued writing stories in the hopes of getting them published.

Lewis Carroll is well-known for his imaginative story about a girl's underground adventures, but did you know that Alice was actually based on a real person? While on a picnic, Lewis amused his friend's children with one of his own fairy tales and then agreed to write down the story for little Alice Liddell. The girl loved his story and Carroll was encouraged by friends to have it published. His book became a bestseller and his fame soon spread around the world. Later on he wrote other successful books.

Although he didn't really enjoy all the attention he received, he earned a lot of money from his books. Interestingly, despite his success, his life hardly changed at all and he continued to teach in the same university until 1881. His main work as a mathematician should not be forgotten because he developed many new ideas. He also had a talent as an inventor and created things, such as a steering device for a velociam (tricycle) and an early version of Scrabble.

"Without a plan, it doesn't matter which way you're going."
Lewis Carroll

Lauren Child

- **Born:** 29th November 1965
- **To:** Present
- **Place of birth:** Berkshire, UK
- **First book:** *Clarice Bean, That's Me* (1999)
- **Best-known book:** *Charlie and Lola* series (2000)

The daughter of two teachers and the middle child of three girls, Lauren grew up named Helen until she changed her name to a new one that she preferred. She left school to study Fine Art in Manchester and London. She describes her twenties as an uninspired time of her life doing various creative but badly paid jobs such as painting china and murals. She even started her own company called 'Chandeliers for People', making lampshades.

In 1995, Lauren woke up on her thirtieth birthday and decided she wanted to do something better with her life having felt quite lost during the previous decade. She began writing and in 1999, her first two books were published. Almost immediately, her books began receiving lots of awards such as several **Nestlé Smarties** book prizes. She received the **Kate Greenaway** medal for the first book of the *Charlie and Lola* series in 2000. Combining quirky characters, simple storylines and an unusual style of collaged illustration, Lauren's books provided a new style for readers that quickly became popular. In 2005, *Charlie and Lola* was launched as a TV series that is still popular with younger children today.

As **Children's Laureate** from 2017 to 2019, Lauren's aim was to bring together art, television and children's literature, and she has done this very successfully.

> *"We were given: Two hands to hold. Two legs to walk.*
> *Two eyes to see. Two ears to listen. But why only one heart?*
> *Because the other one was given to someone else. For us to find."*
> Lauren Child

Roald Dahl

- **Born:** 13th September 1916
- **Died:** 23rd November 1990
- **Place of birth:** Llandaff, Cardiff
- **First book:** *Gremlins* (1943)
- **Best-known book:** *Charlie and the Chocolate Factory* (1964)

Roald Dahl is one of the most famous authors of all time. He has written 39 books and his works have been translated into 34 languages.

His parents were both Norwegian. Roald had three sisters as well as a half-sister and half-brother from his father's first marriage. Sadly, Roald's sister and dad both died when he was three. As a child, Roald attracted trouble and was once caned for putting a dead mouse in a jar of sweets at the local sweetshop! His father always wanted him to have an English education so Roald headed off to his first boarding school, aged nine. He was extremely homesick but kept this secret when he wrote to his mother every week. At his second boarding school in Repton, the Cadbury's factory sent chocolate for the pupils to test. Maybe this was where he got the idea for his book, *Charlie and the Chocolate Factory*?

At the age of seventeen, once he had finished school, Roald Dahl joined the Shell Petroleum Company and eventually worked in Kenya and Tanzania. This was where he applied to become a fighter pilot at the outbreak of World War 2. During this time, when he was flying a fighter plane, he crash-landed in the Libyan desert and, after dragging himself from the blazing wreckage, spent six months recovering from a skull fracture, a crushed nose and temporary blindness.

Roald suffered from severe, on-going headaches and was eventually sent back to his mum in Buckinghamshire where he then became an instructor for the **RAF**. In 1942, Roald was persuaded to work for the **British Embassy** in Washington DC. He carried out various roles including working as an undercover agent. It was during this period that Roald Dahl began writing in his spare time.

Sometime after the war ended, Roald met American actress Patricia Neal and they married in New York City in 1953. They had five children. When his son Theo was a baby, his pushchair was hit by a New York taxi, which left him with **hydrocephalus**. Roald Dahl got involved in the engineering of a valve used to treat this condition.

It was when his children were small that Dahl wrote many of his well-known books such as *James and the Giant Peach* and *Charlie and the Chocolate Factory*. However, this was a difficult time for Roald as his seven-year-old daughter Olivia died from measles and later his wife suffered with poor health. Roald and Patricia divorced in 1983 and he married Felicity Crosland, a British film producer in the same year.

Many of Dahl's books were written in his little hut at the end of the garden as there were always children or vacuum cleaners disturbing him in the house. He would set up his ideal "writing nest": a comfortable chair with a blanket over him; his footstool in exactly the right spot; six sharpened pencils and a flask nearby. When Roald was making notes for his books, he always used yellow paper and would spend up to four and a half hours writing in his magical, fantasy world. His books are known for being imaginative and he invented five hundred new words, such as splendiferous, gloriumptious and biffsquiggled. In fact there is even a Roald Dahl dictionary. His partnership with illustrator Quentin Blake brought the fictional worlds in his books to life.

It was a sad day all over the world in November 1990 when Roald Dahl died from a rare blood disease. Since then, his legacy has continued with a great number of books, films and shows being released, and many seriously ill children are supported through his Marvellous Children's Charity.

"A little nonsense now and then, is cherished by the wisest men."
Roald Dahl

Charles Dickens

- **Born:** 7th February 1812
- **Died:** 9th June 1870
- **Place of birth:** Portsea Island, Portsmouth
- **First book:** *Sketches by Boz* (1836)
- **Best-known book:** *Oliver Twist* (1838)

Charles John Huffam Dickens was the second oldest in a family of eight children. Unfortunately, his parents and the four youngest children had to spend time in a London prison because his father owed money. As a 12-year-old, Charles had to leave school and work in a dangerous and unhealthy factory to earn a wage. This made him very aware of how awful **poverty** was for many Victorian families. After his father's debt had been repaid, thanks to a **legacy**, Charles was able to return to school.

By 1828 Charles had become a newspaper reporter in one of London's law courts. He became skilled at listening, watching and writing about what he saw, and he soon gathered a lot of useful information about Victorian life. He decided to use his notes to write stories to earn some extra money. He also realised that **serialising** his work kept his readers interested and tempted them to buy more of his work, which gave him a regular wage.

Dickens quickly became a popular author who began writing a mixture of longer stories and **pamphlets** containing messages about the terrible lives of poor people. In 1835 he became the editor of a monthly magazine in which he began serialising his new story *Oliver Twist*, writing up to 90 pages a month. Dickens continued publishing his stories and by now many of them had been turned into plays, which allowed many **illiterate** people to enjoy them too. However, not all his writing was serialised and *A Christmas Carol* was published as a complete book in 1843.

By the time he was 24, Dickens was a smart, wealthy man and was married to Catherine Hogarth, a Scottish woman. Together they had ten children, nine of whom survived to adulthood. Dickens worked very hard for children's rights and to convince important adults about the need for schools. He also used his influence to improve conditions for poor people. He eventually died at the age of 58 but his books are still enjoyed 150 years later.

"We never tire of the friendships we form with books."
Charles Dickens

Berlie Doherty

- **Born:** 6th November 1943
- **To:** Present
- **Place of birth:** Knotty Ash, Liverpool
- **First book:** *How Green You Are!* (1982)
- **Best-known book:** *Street Child* (1993)

© Richard Harland Photography

Encouraged by her father, Berlie Doherty wrote for the children's pages of a newspaper from the age of 5 years old until she turned 14. After studying at three universities, Durham, Liverpool and Sheffield, Berlie worked as a social worker and as a teacher. Later she spent two years writing and producing schools' programmes for BBC Radio Sheffield.

In 1983, once her three children were at school, she decided to become a full-time writer. She has written books in very different genres for both children and adults, including fantasy, poetry, drama, works associated with music, and novels.

She often works with children and teenagers when developing her novels, because she says, "Children are the experts and I can always learn from them." For example, her research for *Spellhorn* included extensive work with a group of blind children attending a school in Sheffield.

She loves writing poems and plays for radio too. She has adapted two of her novels for television: *White Peak Farm* for BBC1 and *Children of Winter* for Channel 4. As well as many other awards, Berlie has won the **Carnegie Medal** twice. Berlie now lives in the Peak District. She usually writes from a little barn which looks out across fields of sheep, inside by a big log fire, or outdoors perched on a stone by the river.

"Maybe we want to burn off across the horizon, into space, perhaps, into some unknown territory and meet ourselves out there."

Berlie Doherty

Julia Donaldson

- **Born:** 16th September 1948
- **To:** Present
- **Place of birth:** Hampstead, London
- **First book:** *A Squash and a Squeeze* (1993)
- **Best known book:** *The Gruffalo* (1999)

Julia was born after World War 2 and her family bought a three-storey Victorian house where she lived with her parents, her sister Mary, her aunt and uncle, two cousins and her grandma. This might be where she got the idea to write *A Squash and a Squeeze!* It was an interesting childhood full of music, poetry, theatre and different languages. By the age of nineteen, Julia had a good grasp of three European languages and went to study Drama and French at Bristol University.

After university, Julia married her husband Malcolm and ran Saturday-morning theatre workshops for children. She also wrote many songs for BBC TV. Having had three children, Julia later volunteered in her son's primary school, helping pupils develop their reading skills.

In 1991, a publisher asked if they could turn Julia's *A Squash and a Squeeze* song into a book with illustrations by the German artist, Axel Scheffler, something that was the start of a long and successful partnership. As a result, Julia began to adapt her love of poems and music to writing children's books. She and Axel went on to create many of the best-selling picture books of all time, many of which have now been animated for television.

As well as her projects with Axel, Julia has also written countless other books, plays and poems, and was chosen as **Children's Laureate** between 2011 and 2013. She is still writing new books for children to love.

"I opened a book and in I strode. Now nobody can find me."

Julia Donaldson

Anne Fine

- **Born:** 7th December 1947
- **To:** Present
- **Place of birth:** Leicester, England
- **First book:** *The Summer House Loon* (1978)
- **Best-known book:** *Diary of A Killer Cat* (1994)

As a child, the authors that inspired Anne to read were Anthony Buckeridge, who wrote the *Jennings* series of books, and Richmal Crompton's *Just William* series about the 11-year-old William. Both of these authors wrote about mischievous boys and their gangs. Once she became a teenager, however, Anne enjoyed books by Geoffrey Trease and Henry Treece, both of whom wrote historical stories which were carefully researched and accurate.

Anne attended Northampton High School and then studied politics and history at the University of Warwick. She was a teacher for a short while and also worked for Oxfam before beginning her writing career.

As an author she says that she always works in the same way, i.e., early in the morning before getting up, using a laptop or a pencil and paper, with lots of tea to drink, and always in absolute silence. She doesn't like talking about anything that she is writing or letting anyone look at her work until it is almost completely finished.

Anne has written more than seventy children's books including some that have won medals and awards. She has been Children's Author of the Year twice. Her book *Alias Madame Doubtfire* was published in 1987, and the story was made into the film *Mrs Doubtfire* in 1993.

Anne became the UK's second Children's Laureate (2001–03) and in 2003 she was appointed **OBE** by the Queen "for services to literature". During her time as the **Children's Laureate** she worked hard to encourage children to start their own home libraries with second-hand books because she realised that many families owned very few books. Anne says that she prefers reading other people's books, especially to her grandchildren, to writing her own because it is such a pleasure to re-read her favourites with children.

"My favourite piece of advice is from the poet Philip Larkin who said, 'Write the book that you yourself would most like to read, but that nobody else has bothered to write for you.'"

Anne Fine

Anthony Horowitz

- **Born:** 5th April 1955
- **To:** Present
- **Place of birth:** Stanmore, London
- **First book:** *Enter Fredrick K. Bower* (1979)
- **Best-known book:** *Alex Rider* series (2000)

Anthony described his father Mark as someone who treated his family very coldly and distantly. Mark Horowitz never encouraged Anthony's talents and told him that he would never be a writer; the only thing that Anthony really wanted to be. As a young boy, Anthony enjoyed the Tintin stories and later on the Sherlock Holmes mysteries and the James Bond books.

Anthony and his family lived in a huge mansion and they were looked after by servants. The children were supervised by their cruel grandmother when their parents were away. Anthony was unhappy and overweight as a child and was teased at school. He was sent to a private boarding **prep school** in north London where he was very unhappy and was physically beaten by the head teacher. He was moved to an expensive boarding school in Rugby where he was equally miserable at first. However, he later became more settled when three teachers encouraged his interest in creative subjects. To avoid being teased by bullies, Anthony used to tell them stories at night-time. Doing this allowed him to escape his unhappiness but it also encouraged him to write.

When he left school, he spent a **gap year** in Australia working as a cowboy to see more of the world. He travelled back to England overland through different foreign countries, and he has said that he learned more in those years than in the previous ten. Anthony studied English literature and art history at the University of York before working as a **copywriter**. In 1985, he decided to concentrate on his writing, although he also contributed to various television programmes including the Hercule Poirot programmes, and he created both *Midsomer Murders* and *Foyle's War*. Horowitz has written lots of novels and scripts including series such as *Groosham Grange*, *The Diamond Brothers*, *The Power of Five* and *Alex Rider*, all for young adults. Horowitz says that he is proudest of his *Alex Rider* teen spy series because it has inspired a love of reading in so many young people.

Anthony has won a great many awards for his books. In 2008 he was made the UK's first Champion Author for his work with Youth Offenders and Looked After Children. He is also a **patron** of the child protection charity, Kidscape, and the Home-Start charity in Suffolk. In 2014, he was awarded the **OBE** for services to literature.

"The only time when I'm totally happy is when I'm writing."
Anthony Horowitz

Dick King-Smith

- **Born:** 27th March 1922
- **Died:** 4th January 2011
- **Place of birth:** Bitton, Gloucestershire
- **First book:** *The Foxbusters* (1978)
- **Best-known book:** *The Sheep-Pig* (1983)

Although Dick King-Smith was named Ronald Gordon at birth, his family began to call him "Dick" after he called birds dicky-birds. Dick was educated at a **prep school** and then at the famous Marlborough College, Wiltshire.

In 1940 he began a farming **apprenticeship**, a job for which he was paid £1 per week. He met his future wife Myrle when they were both 14 years old, and they married three years later. During World War 2 Dick served in Italy as an officer until he was injured by an exploding hand grenade and sent back to England.

He spent 20 enjoyable years running two farms with his wife and raising their three children. Although he and his wife loved their farming years, neither of their farms were financially successful.

In 1972, he and his oldest daughter began to study to become teachers at a university in Bristol. Once he was qualified, Dick taught for seven years, firstly eight-year-olds and later younger children because he was not considered good enough to teach the older ones maths.

By then, recognising that children loved his stories, he started his writing career. Although many of his stories are about animals, some of his books also have human characters who make his readers think about things differently. His fame quickly spread beyond his stories. He and his animals, especially his dog Dodo, also became stars of three television series.

He is best known for *The Sheep-Pig* (1983) that was translated into many other languages and adapted into the film *Babe* in 1995. After the success of *The Sheep-Pig*, Dick went on to win many other awards and was appointed **OBE** in 2010 for his services to children's literature.

"Failures are merely dress rehearsals for success."
Dick King-Smith

C.S. Lewis

- **Born:** 29th November 1898
- **Died:** 22nd November 1963
- **Place of birth:** Belfast, Northern Ireland
- **First book:** *Spirits in Bondage* (1919)
- **Best-known book:** *The Lion, The Witch and the Wardrobe* (1950)

Clive Staples Lewis, known as C.S. Lewis, was called Jack during everyday life. He was a **biblical scholar**, a university teacher and a well-known writer. *The Chronicles of Narnia* are his most popular children's books and it has been estimated that over 100 million copies of these books have been sold in 47 languages. They have also been adapted for radio, television, stage and cinema.

Lewis and his older brother, Warren, grew up in Belfast, in a rich and educated family. As little boys the brothers spent a lot of time creating and illustrating their own stories and making small model figures and **dioramas** for their fantasy world.

The boys were both home-schooled until 1905 when Warren was sent to a boarding school in England. Sadly, their mother died unexpectedly in 1908 and "Jack" was sent to join Warren at the same school; a school where the pupils were mistreated by the headmaster, a situation which later led to the school's closure.

Lewis went to Oxford University in summer 1917 but almost immediately World War I began. He fought in the army for a short while before being injured in battle. He returned to his university to study Greek and Latin literature, philosophy and ancient history, and English. Lewis worked there for the next thirty years writing many books, mainly for adults, and giving lectures explaining Christianity. In 1954 he moved to a post at Magdalene College, Cambridge, but retained strong links with Oxford.

Whilst working in Oxford he lived in a house that he, his brother and another two friends purchased.

Between 1930 and 1945, Lewis was part of a small friendly literary discussion group of which J.R.R. Tolkien was also a member. Tolkien, who like Lewis was a professor at the university, went on to write the famous fantasy stories *The Hobbit* and *The Lord of the Rings*.

The Lion, the Witch and the Wardrobe, the first book in Lewis's *Chronicles of Narnia* series, was published in 1950. He wrote these seven books to help children consider many of the Christian ideas that he believed in.

In 1952, whilst he was working at Cambridge University, Joy Davidman Gresham, a divorced American fan of his books, came to visit him. She and Lewis fell in love and eventually married, with Joy and her two young sons moving into Lewis's home. The couple enjoyed four happy years of marriage together before, sadly, Joy died when she was only 45 years old. Although Jack was heartbroken by his wife's death, he carried on looking after his stepsons and even wrote a book for adults about the sadness of losing someone you love.

In 1961 he became ill and decided to retire from the university. He enjoyed another few years of life but died just before his 65th birthday.

> *"A children's story that can only be enjoyed by children is not a good children's story in the slightest."*
>
> C.S. Lewis

Michelle Magorian

- **Born:** 6th November 1947
- **To:** Present
- **Place of birth:** Southsea, Portsmouth
- **First book:** *Goodnight Mr Tom* (1981)
- **Best-known book:** *Goodnight Mr Tom* (1981)

Michelle was born in Portsmouth but moved to Singapore and then Australia as a child before returning to the UK at the age of 9. Her intention was always to be an actress and she trained at the Rose Bruford College of Speech and Drama and at Marcel Marceau's L'Ecole Internationale de Mime in Paris. "Mikki" Magorian was her stage name.

When she was 24 she became interested in children's books, and decided to write one herself. She wrote her first book in between her acting commitments, which is why it took her several years to finish it. Later she joined a writing class and shared her manuscript for *Goodnight Mr Tom* with the other people, who suggested that she should try and have it published. Kestrel Books published it in 1981.

The book was a great success and 1.2 million copies were sold. The book has received various awards and commendations and it was turned into a film and a musical of the same name. It has been translated into twelve languages, the latest being Chinese. It is a very popular story that teaches children about life as an evacuee. Michelle has also written several other stories and two collections of poetry, and she continues to write amazing books.

"I'd rather be happy and odd than miserable and ordinary."
Michelle Magorian

David McKee

- **Born:** 2nd January 1935
- **To:** Present
- **Place of birth:** Tavistock, Devon
- **First book:** *Two Can Toucan* (1964)
- **Best-known book:** *Not Now, Bernard* (1980)

Like many people in the early 1900s, David's parents left school when they were 14 years old. His mum became a servant in a manor house in Tavistock and his dad, a gardener's boy in the same large house.

By the time David was able to read, his parents were too poor to buy books and books were in short supply due to World War 2. However, after attending his local primary school, David progressed to Tavistock Grammar School.

From the late 1940s, most young men were compelled to do a period of **National Service** and as a result David served as an instructor in the Royal Army Educational Corps.

He followed this in 1950 by studying at Plymouth College of Art, selling some of his cartoons during this time to earn extra money.

Next, he decided to study for a second degree at the College of Art in London and it was while he was studying there that he wrote and illustrated his first book which was published in 1964. He was praised for his unusual style of art in his next book, *Bronto's Wings*, about a dinosaur who wanted to fly. As a result, the BBC started using some of his characters in their TV shows. This led to them creating a series using his books and these episodes earned McKee a permanent place in children's fiction. Most of his books, including those about *Elmer the Elephant* and *Mr Benn*, and *Not Now, Bernard*, have remained extremely popular even today.

David, who has a daughter, two sons and three grandchildren, lives in Marseille, France, with his second wife, Bakhta.

> *"It's as though you, as the writer, don't create the words of your story.*
> *It's more that you listen to them as they are waiting to be told*
> *and you write them down."*
> David McKee

A. A. Milne

- **Born:** 18th January 1882
- **Died:** 31st January 1956
- **Place of birth:** Kilburn, London
- **First book:** *The Red House Mystery* (1922)
- **Best-known book:** *The House at Pooh Corner* (1928)

Alan Alexander Milne was an English author, best known for his much-loved tales of Winnie-the-Pooh and Christopher Robin, and also for various poems. As a child, he attended a small, private school run by his father. One of his teachers there was H.G. Wells who became a famous author as well.

Although he studied maths at Cambridge University, Milne went on to become a writer after he graduated. He wrote many plays and novels before Winnie-the-Pooh. He was inspired by his son Christopher Robin, and his soft toy collection, to write stories set in a forest near where he lived.

Even though he was an astonishing author, the end of A.A. Milne's life was quite sad for a number of reasons. He felt he wasn't taken seriously as an author because people thought his books were just for children. Also, his relationship with his son was not the greatest as Christopher Robin didn't appreciate having his name in the various books. Sadly, A.A. Milne suffered a **stroke** in 1952 and spent the last four years of his life in a wheelchair.

After his death, Walt Disney productions bought the rights to use his characters and stories and went on to produce over fifteen feature films, a number of TV programmes and billions of dollars' worth of merchandise.

"Promise me you'll always remember: You're braver than you believe, and stronger than you seem, and smarter than you think."

A.A. Milne.

Michael Morpurgo

- **Born:** 5th October 1943
- **To:** Present
- **Place of birth:** St Albans, Hertfordshire
- **First book:** *It Never Rained* (1974)
- **Best-known book:** *War Horse* (1982)

© Phil Crow

Although his name was Michael Bridge until he was 5 years old, after his mother's remarriage to Jack Morpurgo, Michael and his older brother Pieter began to use the Morpurgo surname. Their birth father, Tony, and their mother, Kippe, were both actors. The boys' new stepfather eventually became an editor, a university professor and a writer. The only contact that the two brothers had with their real father had been when they were pre-school children and Michael was 19 years old before he learned anything about Tony Bridge.

Once his biological parents were divorced, his birth father emigrated to Canada and was never mentioned again within the new stepfamily; in fact Michael hadn't ever seen a photograph of Tony. However, on Christmas Eve 1962, when he was 19 years old, and while he was watching a TV version of the Charles Dickens story *Great Expectations* with his mother, she pointed out his real father to him on the screen. Tony was playing the role of the escaped convict Abel Magwitch. As a result of this discovery, Michael and his father were finally able to meet.

Michael and his brother were evacuated to Northumberland during World War 2, and then, after the war, the family moved to London, where the boys often played on bombsites. Later the family moved to Bradwell-on-Sea, Essex.

From age 7 to 13, Michael attended a boys' boarding school in Sussex. The discipline was very strict, and the pupils were often beaten, something that led Michael to develop a temporary **stutter**. Later on, however, he was able to make use of some of these unhappy experiences in his book *The Butterfly Lion*.

From 14 to 19 years of age he attended The King's School, a famous private school in Canterbury and although he was not very successful in his studies, he enjoyed rugby and singing. He was head boy for a time.

As Michael didn't do well at school, his stepfather persuaded him to sign up at an army training centre. However, Michael quickly realised that he was not interested in becoming a soldier and he gave up his training after nine months. In 1963, he married his girlfriend Clare, who was expecting their first baby. He completed a period of **National Service** and later graduated from King's College, London, with a degree in English, French and philosophy.

Between 1967 and 1977, Michael taught in several primary schools and at a private **prep school** in Cambridge. During this time his wife had also become a teacher. Once it became clear to him that many of his pupils loved his stories he developed **parallel careers** as a teacher and a children's author. As Michael and his wife became busier, they began to want a less stressful life. They looked for ways to improve the lives of inner-city children outside of their classrooms. This was how the Farms for City Children project started.

Clare Morpurgo used a **legacy** from her father to start the charity. The Morpurgos **leased** a small farm and its fields in Devon, plus a nearby cottage for them to live in, and began welcoming groups of city pupils for a week's practical experience on the farm. Today there are three farms that offer schoolchildren this opportunity. Michael saw how the children responded and collected lots of useful information to use in his future books.

In addition he also met an old man in a local pub who had been a **horse artillery soldier** during World War I who talked about the dreadful experiences involving horses used in battles. Soon after, Michael heard a very shy boy with a bad **stammer** talking to a horse in a stable. Seeing the love between the boy and the horse was enough to convince Michael that he needed to write the book *War Horse* about the experiences of farm horses at war. *War Horse* was a great success as a book; so much so that it was adapted for radio, as a stage play and a film.

Michael has written more than 100 children's books and stories, some of which have been made into operatic, film, television and ballet productions and been seen and heard across around the world. With Ted Hughes, the famous poet who was a close friend of the Morpurgos, Michael worked hard to create a new award entitled **Children's Laureate**. Michael has earned a great deal of recognition including holding the position of Children's Laureate between 2003 and 2005. Both he and Clare were appointed **MBE** in 1999, with Michael being appointed **OBE** in 2006 and made a **Knight** by the Queen in 2018 for his services to literature and his charity work. However, despite being recognised in so many different ways, Michael has said that creating the Farms for City Children charity with his wife has been his greatest achievement.

"The most important thing is to live an interesting life.
Keep your eyes, ears and heart open. Talk to people and visit interesting
places, and don't forget to ask questions."
Michael Morpurgo

Beatrix Potter

- **Born:** 28th July 1866
- **Died:** 22nd December 1943
- **Place of birth:** West Brompton, London
- **First book:** *The Tale of Peter Rabbit* (1902)
- **Best-known book:** *The Tale of Peter Rabbit* (1902)

Helen Beatrix Potter was a writer, an illustrator, a **natural scientist** and a **conservationist** who grew up with her younger brother Bertram and her wealthy parents in a very smart London suburb. The children led very **sheltered lives** and didn't have many friends. However, because their parents were artistic and interested in nature, they allowed their children to keep various small animals indoors, including mice, rabbits, a hedgehog and some bats. Beatrix loved the countryside and whenever the Potter family was on holiday in Scotland or the English Lake District she sketched and painted many of the plants and animals that she saw.

As she grew older, Beatrix used to send illustrated letters to the children of her former governess. As a result, Beatrix's mother suggested – much later on – that these amusing letters could be turned into a children's book. In 1901, Miss Potter **self-published** a small number of copies of a book about four naughty rabbits for her family and friends. The following year, however, the publishing company who had previously rejected her story, reconsidered it and decided to print copies of it for sale to the public, a decision that led to Beatrix becoming famous. This was the start of her full-time career of writing and illustrating children's books.

During the next 57 years, as she became a successful and wealthy author, she also purchased sixteen Lake District farms to protect the beautiful countryside in which they stood. When Beatrix died, she left almost all the property she owned to the National Trust.

More than two dozen of her books were published, many of which continue to sell throughout the world, translated into different languages. Some of her stories are continuing to be retold through songs, films, ballet, and animations. Parts of her life have also been highlighted through films.

"There is something delicious about writing the first words of a story because you never quite know where they'll take you."

Beatrix Potter

Philip Pullman

- **Born:** 19th October 1946
- **To:** Present
- **Place of birth:** Norwich, Norfolk
- **First book:** *The Haunted Storm* (1972)
- **Best-known book:** *Northern Lights* (1995)

Philip Pullman's mother, Audrey, was once a **WAAF** Officer. Sadly, his father, Alfred, who was an **RAF** pilot, died whilst flying a plane when Philip was eight years old. A year afterwards, his mother married another RAF pilot and because they were sent to Australia, his new family - including several half-siblings - lived in Adelaide for about two years. Later on, the family was transferred to Harlech, North Wales.

When Philip was once asked once about his favourite book as a child, he named *The Magic Pudding* by Norman Lindsay. Later he added *Grimm's Fairy Tales*, Sherlock Holmes by Arthur Conan Doyle, and the *Superman* and *Batman* comic books as stories that inspired him. Philip enjoyed poetry from an early age and feels that this and the Welsh countryside made him aware that ordinary and extraordinary things can exist together, a fact that has influenced his writing.

Having gained an English degree from Oxford University, Philip stayed in Oxford to teach in various middle schools. He got married in 1970. Whilst teaching, he wrote his first school play and began to work on a novel, *The Haunted Storm*. This earned him a Young Writer's Award in 1972. Over the next few years, he continued teaching whilst writing plays and novels. He eventually wrote his first children's book, *Count Karlstein* (1982) and stopped teaching full-time in 1986.

He took a part-time job at Westminster College, Oxford, and whilst still creating plays for schools he also began work on a series of novels, with the first book in the *His Dark Materials* series, *The Northern Lights* (known as *The Golden Compass* in North America) being published in 1995. He became increasingly popular and as a result won a huge number of awards for his work, the most special one perhaps being made a **Knight** in 2019.

His books have been translated into many languages and he is known internationally as one of the best writers of our time. His writing has been made into plays, films, screen and radio material, and even an opera!

"Tell stories. To children. To each other.
A story will enchant and beguile and bewitch."

Philip Pullman

Arthur Ransome

- **Born:** 18th January 1884
- **Died:** 3rd June 1967
- **Place of birth:** Leeds, England
- **First book:** *The Child's Book of the Seasons* (1906)
- **Best known book:** *Swallows and Amazons* (1930)

Arthur Michell Ransome was the eldest child, with a brother and two sisters. They lived in Leeds where his father was Professor of History at Yorkshire College (which later became Leeds University) and his mother was a gifted watercolour artist.

When he was 9 years old, he was sent to a boarding school in Windermere in the Lake District but he was not happy there. Arthur was not very successful at his schoolwork, but it was later discovered that he was extremely short-sighted which may have contributed to this. However, his first housemaster encouraged Ransome to write. Arthur and his family enjoyed holidays in the Lake District where he learnt to row and fish. Sadly, his father died when Ransome was just thirteen.

After briefly studying chemistry at Yorkshire College, Ransome decided to move to London to become a writer. He married his first wife, Ivy, and they had a daughter, but they later divorced. His second marriage was to a Russian woman called Evgenia. During his life, he lived in England, Russia, Latvia and Estonia, and wrote about the war and revolution in Russia. The English government was suspicious of his links with the new Russian leaders and some suspected him of being a double agent.

The couple settled in Arthur's beloved Lake District where he wrote many children's books, one of which won the very first **Carnegie Medal**. His love of nature, fishing and sailing is clearly reflected in his stories.

> *"When a thing's done, it's done, and if it's not done right,*
> *do it differently next time."*
> Arthur Ransome

J.K. Rowling

- **Born:** 31st July 1965
- **To:** Present
- **Place of birth**: Yate, Gloucestershire
- **First book:** *Harry Potter and the Philosopher's Stone* (2001)
- **Best-known book:** *Harry Potter* series (2001–2007)

Joanne Kathleen Rowling, better known as Jo, was a bookworm and wrote her first story aged six. She attended several schools and always enjoyed English. As a quiet, not very athletic child, she would write stories for her friends at lunchtimes. Her whole family enjoyed the outdoors, and Jo and her sister Dianne loved being able to wander unsupervised around the countryside.

At Exeter University, Jo studied French and Classics, and once received a £50 library fine for overdue books. Her knowledge of Ancient Greek and Latin helped her invent the spells when she wrote the *Harry Potter* stories.

She dreamed up the idea for Harry Potter while trapped on a delayed train, and over the next five years, she mapped out the whole series. During this time, she moved to Portugal to teach English. There she married and had a daughter, Jessica. In 1993, Jo returned to live in Edinburgh with her baby and the first three chapters of *Harry Potter and the Philosopher's Stone*. As a single parent, she worked as a French teacher but continued to write her book in her spare time, often when her daughter was asleep.

When Rowling finally finished the book, the manuscript was rejected twelve times before she found a **publisher**. However, her efforts paid off because now over 500 million *Harry Potter* books have been sold and she has become the richest author in the world. Later on, Warner Brothers proposed turning the books into a series of movies. Jo agreed and the films made $7.7 million. With never-ending merchandise, two theme parks, a Warner Brothers studio tour and even a theatre production, *Harry Potter* has created a $21 billion business.

After *Harry Potter*, Rowling chose to write books on crime, a topic she had always loved as a reader. Instead of using her own name, she used the **pseudonym** Robert Galbraith because she wanted the books to be judged on their own merit and not be compared to *Harry Potter*.

J.K. Rowling now lives in Edinburgh with her second husband, Neil Murray, and has three children. She does a lot of work for charities including her own charity, 'Lumos', which is named after the light-giving spell from the wizarding world. It helps some of the eight million children across the world who are orphaned, just like Tom Riddle and Harry Potter.

"Happiness can be found, even in the darkest of times,
if one only remembers to turn on the light."
J.K. Rowling

Jeremy Strong

- **Born:** 18th November 1949
- **To:** Present
- **Place of birth:** Eltham, London
- **First book:** *Smith's Tail* (1978)
- **Best-known book:** *The Hundred-Mile-an-Hour Dog* (1995)

Jeremy had a bumpy start to life because he fell out of a bedroom window as a toddler. He landed outside his house and lay unconscious on the ground. He woke up in a hospital bed with a massive headache and a broken right arm. However, he went on to do lots of great things.

When he was a child, he liked Rudyard Kipling's books and Enid Blyton's *Famous Five* series. As a boy, his family listened to lots of radio. Jeremy found himself enjoying the incredibly silly *Goon Show*. As well as writing the scripts for the show, a comedian called Spike Milligan also wrote books for children that were full of crazy humour. Milligan was a comic genius who used sound effects in his shows as well as words. He inspired Jeremy to write.

Although he started writing stories and poems when he was child, it wasn't until Jeremy was 18 that he started writing books for adults. Unfortunately, none of these early books were published; in fact he didn't get his first book published until he was nearly 30. But, once he realised that he loved writing funny stories, he started to write for children. Eventually, when he was 42 years old, he decided to leave his teaching career. This was just before his book *There's a Viking in my Bed* went on sale. Jeremy uses his past experiences, his childhood and his work as a teacher for story ideas but says that anything can inspire you to write a book. He spends the largest part of each day in a shed at the bottom of his garden where he has all the things that he needs for writing.

Since Jeremy began writing, he has had over 100 books published and has won lots of awards. Several of his books have been adapted for BBC Radio. Although most of his books are for confident readers, Jeremy regularly writes stories for children who have **dyslexia**. After thirty years of marriage and two children, Jeremy and his first wife decided to separate. Two years later however, he remarried and he is still writing books.

> *"It made me feel that bad things could happen,*
> *but they didn't have to stay bad."*
>
> Jeremy Strong

David Walliams

- **Born:** 20th August 1971
- **To:** Present
- **Place of birth:** Wimbledon, London
- **First book:** *The Boy In The Dress* (2008)
- **Best-known book:** *Gangsta Granny* (2011)

David's birth name was David Edward Williams but at 19 he changed his surname to Walliams. When he was a toddler his sister used to dress him up in a bridesmaid's dress, put a handbag on his arm, a fur hat on his head and then parade him along the street in which they lived. David liked dressing up and said that adults used to think this was sweet and often wanted to take photos of him.

At school, he enjoyed books by Dr Seuss and Richard Scarry. He always chose books with lots of illustrations because what he really looked forward to was being able to enjoy the pictures.

After passing his **11+ exam** he went to Reigate Grammar School. David wasn't a sporty child and so he avoided football when ever possible. He describes his younger self as quite shy and says that because he found it hard to make friends he spent quite a lot of time alone in his bedroom. He didn't mind being alone and enjoyed practising characters and voices.

When he was 11 years old, he played the role of Queen Henrietta-Maria in the school production of *All the King's Men*, wearing a floor-length dress. He was used to being teased for being girly, but he was applauded for his success in this part which allowed him to escape his unhappiness by temporarily becoming someone else. Performing in school plays and hearing people laugh made him really happy.

He spent a lot of his spare time at home listening to comedians' performances, learning their lines, writing them down, reciting them and trying to understand what actually makes comedy successful.

Between 1989 and 1992 he studied drama at the University of Bristol. Since then he has become a comedian, a children's writer, a TV and stage actor, a script writer, a talent show judge and a television personality.

During his university holidays he performed with the National Youth Theatre (NYT) but in order to act with them he had to join Equity, the actors' **trade union**. However, because there was already someone called David Williams on the actors' register, he took David Walliams as his stage name. It was while he was acting with the NYT that he met Matt Lucas, who later became his comedy partner.

Walliams has sold almost 40 million copies of his children's books worldwide in 53 different languages and he has been described as "the new Roald Dahl". Some of his books have been adapted into films for television and stage plays.

David married the Dutch model Lara Stone in 2010 but the couple divorced in 2015. However, they had a baby son in 2013 whom they both love. David also lives with a mental health condition called **bipolar disorder**.

David believes that charity work is very important, and his efforts have included long-distance outdoor swimming events that have raised millions of pounds for charities. In 2017 he was appointed **OBE** for his work for charity and the arts.

"In Britain, a cup of tea is the answer to every problem!"
David Walliams

Jacqueline Wilson

- **Born:** 17th December 1945
- **To:** Present
- **Place of birth:** Bath, Somerset
- **First book:** *Ricky's Birthday* (1969)
- **Best-known book:** *The Story of Tracy Beaker* (1991)

Jacqueline's father, Harry, was a technical drawing expert whilst her mother, Biddy, had various jobs. Although Jacqueline was born in Bath she spent most of her childhood in Kingston upon Thames near London.

Jacqueline has said that "her parents were not a very good match for each other but that they continued living together in the family home". Her childhood, she has also said once, "was not a happy one".

From an early age, since she was an only child, she often used her imagination and quickly filled up exercise books with her stories. In fact when she was 9 years old, she wrote a 21-page book called *Meet the Maggots* about a family with seven children. However, it was never published.

At school she became addicted to books and loved reading her stories out loud. As her stories were often unusual, she was not always given good marks for her creative writing. One of her teachers nicknamed her Jacky Daydream, a name she used later as the title of her 2009 autobiography, in which she describes her life as a primary school child.

As a youngster she particularly enjoyed books by the English author Mary Noel Streatfeild but she also liked stories written by American authors including *Little Women* and the *What Katy Did* series.

She passed her **11+ exam** at her second attempt and moved to Coombe Girls' School in New Malden where she passed the equivalent of five or six **GCSEs**. She left school when she was 16 years old because she didn't want to study any longer at that school. Instead she spent a year studying at a **secretarial college** and during this time she sold several of her stories to a publisher. The company then offered her a full-time job writing for *Jackie*, a new magazine for teenage girls. The job was in Scotland which meant that she had to leave home and live in a girls' **hostel**. When she was 19 years old, she married a man from Dundee. They had a daughter when Jacqueline was 21 years old but they separated in 2004.

To begin with, Jacqueline wrote several crime fiction novels for adults before she switched to writing children's books. For many years her early **standalone** books did not sell too well but it was The Story of Tracy Beaker that brought her fame and money. Jacqueline puts the book's success down to its heart-breaking but funny content, and Nick Sharratt's amusing illustrations. This collaboration was the start of a long-lasting partnership.

Jacqueline felt that many of the children's books that she read as a child were about characters from **middle class** families who had kind, reliable mummies and daddies and who lived in nice houses with lovely gardens. Although she says that she loved reading about worlds like these, she remembered thinking that her own life wasn't like that and because of this, she longed to be able to read some much grittier stories, or **grit-lit**, about the hard parts of some children's lives.

Jacqueline was inspired by stories about working-class children such as the One End Street series by Eve Garnett and *The Binkleby's* books by Ursula Moray Williams. Since 1972 she has written over 74 books for children and the fact that she seems to understand young people, the way they live and the problems that they encounter, together with her sense of humour, is probably what has made them so popular.

She has sold over forty million copies of her books, many of which have been translated into other languages and also turned into radio and stage plays as well as television series. Jacqueline has received many prizes and awards including being appointed **OBE** in 2002 for encouraging literacy in schools. In 2008 she was made a **Dame** in further recognition of her efforts.

As a very successful author, she now lives in Kingston-upon-Thames in southern England with her friend Trish and a rescued cat called Jacob.

"I have this belief that children become readers before they can read.
They become hooked on books as a result of being read aloud to as a child."
Jacqueline Wilson

Glossary

11+ exam	An exam to decide whether or not a child attends grammar school
apprenticeship	A low-paid training job
biblical scholar	Someone who studies the Bible
bipolar disorder	A mental health condition that can cause unusually high levels of excitement or sadness
British Embassy	An office representing Britain in a different country
Carnegie Medal	A medal awarded each year to one outstanding book written in English for children and young people
Children's Laureate	A position awarded to a different children's writer or illustrator every two years in celebration of their outstanding achievements
conservationist	Someone who works to protect the natural world
copywriter	Someone who writes the text for advertisements
Dame	A title awarded by the king or queen to a woman who has served her country well in her area of work
diorama	A 3D model
dyslexia	A learning difficulty which affects the skills of reading, writing and spelling
gap year	Time spent out of education or work, used for travel or other experiences
GCSEs	Exams in different subjects that are usually completed at the age of 16.
Grit Lit	A type of story that is focused on real-life difficulties or challenges
horse artillery soldier	A soldier who works with horses in battle
hostel	Inexpensive accommodation for temporary guests
hydrocephalus	A condition where fluid builds up in the brain

illiterate	Unable to read or write
Kate Greenaway Medal	A medal awarded each year to one outstanding illustrator of books for children and young people
Knight	A title awarded by a king or queen to a man who has served his country well in his area of work
leased	Rented or hired for a longer period of time
legacy	A gift of money left to a person after someone's death
MBE	Member of the British Empire. A special award from a king or queen to someone who has served Britain well in their area of work
middle class	Professional working people who are neither poor nor very rich
milliner	Someone who designs and makes hats
National Service	A compulsory period of service for young people often in the armed forces
natural scientist	A person who studies the natural world
Nestlé Smarties book prize	An annual award for children's literature between 1985 and 2007
OBE	Order of the British Empire. A special award from a king or queen to someone who has served Britain well in their area of work
pamphlets	Short information leaflets
parallel career	Working in two careers at the same time
patron	A person who gives money or support to an organisation
pen name	A fictional name used instead of an author's own name
poverty	A lack of money for basic needs
prep school	A private school for 7–13 year olds which charges fees
pseudonym	A fictional name used instead of an author's own name
publisher	A company which turns an author's writing into a printed book

RAF	Royal Air Force
secretarial college	A training college for secretaries.
self-published	A book that the author has paid to have published
serialising	A story released in multiple parts
sheltered lives	Lives protected from trouble or worry
stammer	A speech disorder where words are stuttered
standalone books	Books that are not part of a series
stroke	An illness in which the supply of oxygen to a part of the brain is greatly reduced
trade union	An organisation which supports and protects workers' rights
WAAF	Women's Auxiliary Air Force